Y0-AQW-337

code care

code care

PRAYER POEMS OF A NURSE

MARJORIE GRAY

Ave Maria Press / Notre Dame / Indiana 46556

ISBN: 0-87793-063-5

© 1974 by Ave Maria Press
All rights reserved

Photography: M. E. Kronstein

Printed in the United States of America

To the Teachers and Students
of
St. Michael's School of Nursing
Toronto, Ontario

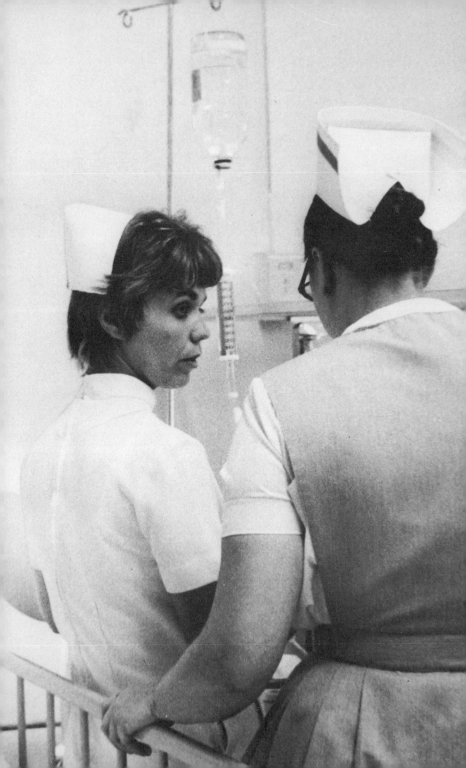

Preface

The thoughts expressed in this book began with the Nursing Profession and will probably never end as long as nurses are nurses. They are like a diary—a daily account of circumstances, thoughts and meditations in the life of a nurse—moments shared with others.

As nurses we have all felt "this way," have nursed the same patients, have been members of the same health teams, have all wondered why we "ever decided to be a nurse," and have sometimes known the answer.

Perhaps this book will help you to recognize yourself. You can read how someone just like you fails sound ideals, is tempted to cater to the perfect patient, and sometimes thinks herself a model only to realize all too quickly that she has more shortcomings than the others combined. We are so much alike even in our differences—children of the same family, daughters of the same Father. It is in this family spirit that these thoughts are shared.

A Nurse's Prayer

Christ,
may we nurses
work with devotion.

May we touch with gentleness;
may we speak with tenderness;
may we listen with our eyes
as well as our ears.

May we smile from the heart;
may we understand with deep
    feeling;
may we know the time to be quiet. . .

the time to laugh,
the time to sympathize,
the time to encourage.

and above all,
may we know
that the time to love
is now!

Lord,
hear our prayer.

An endless parade,
the new admissions.

The old lady, nervous
and not too proud to show it.
The burly cop;
overplayed ease betrays
his anxiety.
The teenager;
eyes silently following
her mother's retreat.
The little child;
the only one true enough
to cry.

Each one suffering
from the fear
of the unknown.

Christ,
there isn't any fear
quite as real—
as real as loneliness!

Let us know that
you are with us
"Even to the end of time."

Bed baths and bedpans,
drainage tubes and specimens!
Lord,
how glamorous the white uniforms
looked
from the distance!

In reality,
the colors are more vivid. . .
red, black, green and amber
and no glamour!

Red used to mean
leaves in autumn,
and black, an "after 5" gown;
green,
the grass in summer. . .

Now
I have eyes to see new sights.
Keep them focused,
Lord,
on Truth.

Health,
you have
an unpurchasable price!

More precious than
the smell of a rose,
the setting sun,
the birth of a child
or perfect love.

You run second
only to Faith.

You were Christ's chosen analogy,
for through healing
he taught salvation.

And so, alas,
without Faith
you are nothing.

"For it is in believing,
that we have eternal life."

I want to feel
what the arthritic feels
when he struggles and strives
just to eat a small meal.

I want to be sensitive
to his needs of self-pride
and patiently wait
while he turns on his side.

I want to understand
his surge of hostility
when I work so efficiently
and flaunt my agility!

Christ,
don't let me deprive him
"of the crumbs from the table."

No wonder he won't smile!
Six months on that stryker;
only 22 years old!

Two hours facing the ceiling,
two hours facing the floor,
motionless. . .
round and round the clock,
day after day,
week after week,
Christ,
that's tough
for a speed car racer!

"What will you have me do?"

Mend his body, Lord,
and give him hope!

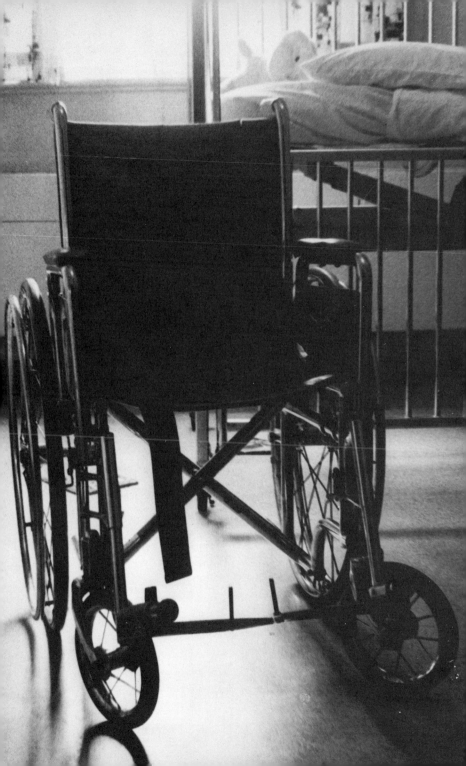

"Dropouts"!
Lord,
how final that word sounds!

All this youth
and energy
and potential;
paralyzed, immobile. . . .

When the turbulence ceases,
Lord,
let them ponder:
We have flown the wrong course,
we have damaged our wings.

"Are we not much more important
than the birds of the field?"

Uplift us from this murky swamp;
help us to see again
the light
of the Son.

Christ,
with all my good intentions
I fail.

I fail my patients
when I ignore
their fear.

I fail my team
when I think
I've done my share.

I fail myself
when I work
without prayer;

and above all
I fail you
in all those things
in which I fail
at all.

"Lord, you are my hope
and my salvation."

I recall
as a student nurse
lectures
on "understanding your patient,"
"emotional support" and
"communication."

I recall
how I silently vowed
with great determination
to measure up to
the "ideal nurse."

I recall
since graduation
slowly but surely
becoming indifferent,
losing sight of
dedication.

Christ,
help me recall
your exhortation
"to put in
all that I have."

Oh Christ,
why me? . . .
that man hasn't bathed in months!
I'm not the only nurse
on this floor. . . .
"She" hasn't done anything
all day!

. . . . well, not really;
but it seems
I really pick them!

hmmm . . . . . now you tell me
about the Good Samaritan.
I hear you.
I hear you!
That's "why me," Lord.

Thank you!
"You know my resting
and my rising."

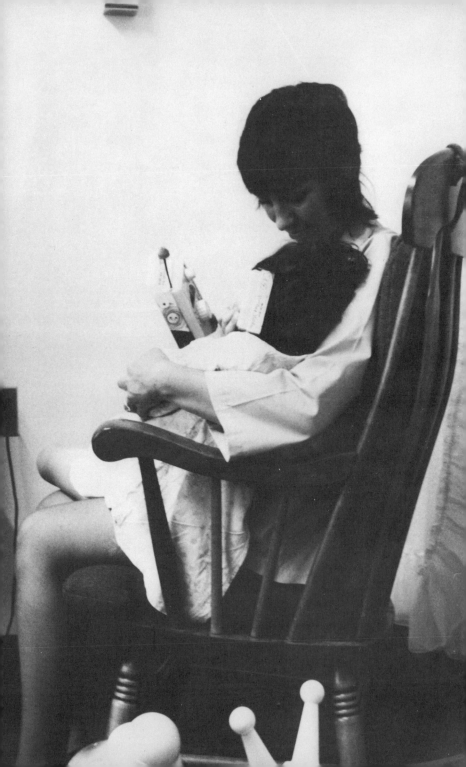

What is success
in nursing?

Is it knowing
how
to make an occupied bed,
or knowing
that a bed is occupied?

Is it patient care,
or caring
for the patient?

Is it knowing
a patient's needs,
or needing
the patient?

What is success
in nursing? . . .

having a love
for your work?
or working
for Love?

Lord,
never let a "patient" become
"the hernia"
"the fistula"
"the colostomy" . . .

Please, God,
let "patient" always be
"person"
to me.

A person
with needs,
a person with feelings,
a person
with a family,
a person
to learn from,
a person
to love.

A person
to help me fulfill
my role
as a person!

Is she really sixty-five?
you'd never guess. . .
why does she want to die?
No home
no family
no husband
but at least she could try. . .
Lord,
she is so lonely.

I wish she knew I cared;
. . . it's no use. . .
she won't even acknowledge
I'm here;
she simply lies and stares.
Wouldn't it help her,
Lord,
to pray?

She just shrugs when I try;
she says
she wants to die.

Lord,
give her the will
to live!

Today, Lord,
I saw a doctor. . .
he was so rough
with a tender incision.

Today, Lord,
I saw a nurse. . .
she was so abrupt
to an undergrad!

Today, Lord,
I saw visitors. . .
they visited each other
instead of the patient!

Today, Lord,
I saw tears
and I passed by!

"Lord, be merciful
to me,
a sinner!"

Only 25, and so depressed!
She's here two weeks now,
an overdose.
I've never seen her smile. . . .

Her chart says she's married—
where is her husband?
There are never any visitors;
surely someone could come
once in a while. . . .

Why not the social workers? . . .
I'm sure someone there
would like to know she's here.
There has to be someone
who cares!

"My soul gives you thanks"
for the idea.

Lord,
fear is clouding
her reasoning.
"Open-heart surgery,"
her only certainty!

She's frightened of X rays,
scared of tests,
scared by doctor's vague
    explanations,
("maybe he told me a lie")
scared by the chaplain's visitation,
("perhaps I am going to die").

Lord,
amid these fears
spread your peace!

"My heart is confident,
O God,
my heart is confident!
I will sing and give you praise,
I will awake at dawn."

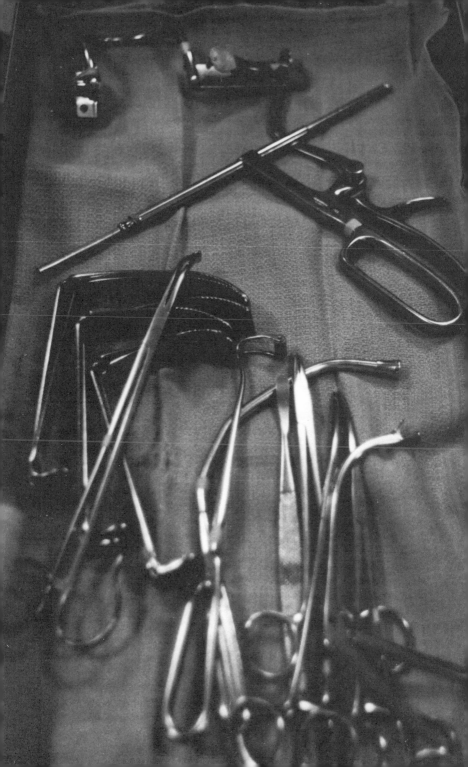

Christ,
I can't stand to see
a suffering child;
it's so hard
to reconcile. . . .

I'd like to scream!
What did he do to deserve this? . . . .
But I know the answer, Lord;
I know this child
has no guilt.

Let me offer his pain
and the grief
of his parents;
unite it, Lord,
to that other
guiltless suffering.

"Suffer the little children
to come
unto me."

The little child
lies motionless;
their hands join for support.
The first time in years
that they shared.

Tears of anguish
on a tiny face
mingled
with their tears
of worry.

Today
all strain forgotten,
in one pain
shared.

"He can make all things
work to the good,
for those who love him."

Drunks and derelicts,
dirt and disease!
Lord,
where are the ideal moments
of neat, groomed nurses,
smiling new mothers
and private rooms with flowers?

Christ, it takes love. . .
so much love!
I need your encouragement.

Tell me over and over again,
"Whatsoever I do
to the least of your brothers,
that I do unto you."

In the "Public Ward"
"good morning"
seems to echo
with a thud.

In the Public Ward
the smile
with which you greet them,
falls like a rainbow
in the mud.

In the Public Ward
forgotten ones
stay a week or two or more,
then they leave
just for another while
to return,
worse than before.

In the Public Ward
you persevere in faith
day after day;
for you recognize
Christ's brothers. . . .
You may be like them
someday.

Why are those curtains
drawn so early this morning?
Christ,
don't tell me he died!
Oh, and I complained last shift
to you. . . .

I was so weary
cleaning up after him;
I silently wished
for a different patient
tomorrow. . . .

Lord,
forgive me
for missing these occasions
to love you.

"You were ill,
and I didn't comfort you."

Sometimes,
it's so hard,
to work with that head nurse!
Christ, don't let her know.

Sometimes,
I grow so tired
of pain
and death
and sorrow.
Christ, don't let it show.

Sometimes,
I come so close
to giving up. . .
Today,
tomorrow. . .
Christ, don't let me go!

Silence
is more
than the absence
of sound.

For the sick
and the lonely,
there can be noise
all around
and there's silence!

Teach me, Lord,
how to speak
without words,
through a touch
or a gesture
to make myself heard
in their silence.

Flowers bedeck her room.
There's no end
to the stream of well-wishing
relatives.

She just lies there. . .
she doesn't speak at all.
They sit,
and they talk
and they watch her. . . . .

She hears them;
she's too tired now
to bother. . . .

"Why did they not sit
and talk to me
these last long years?"

Her face looks peaceful now;
her loneliness is almost over.

"In her Father's house
there are many mansions."

In the world
of senility
everything
is "now";

and for this moment
only
my patient lives,
my patient loves,
my patient laughs,
my patient cries. . .

and I must try
to understand
the confines
of the "present time."

For yesterday
is long forgotten;
and tomorrow
is so far away
as not to be
at all.

Where does man
come closer
to working hand in hand
with God,
than in the O.R.?

Brotherhood,
intensely shared;
Teamwork, trust and education,
no color bar, no prejudice,
the nurses' zeal,
the surgeon's skill,
the anaesthetist's concentration.

Combined and unified,
one goal, one meditation.

In an aura of mystery,
one extension
of God's creation.

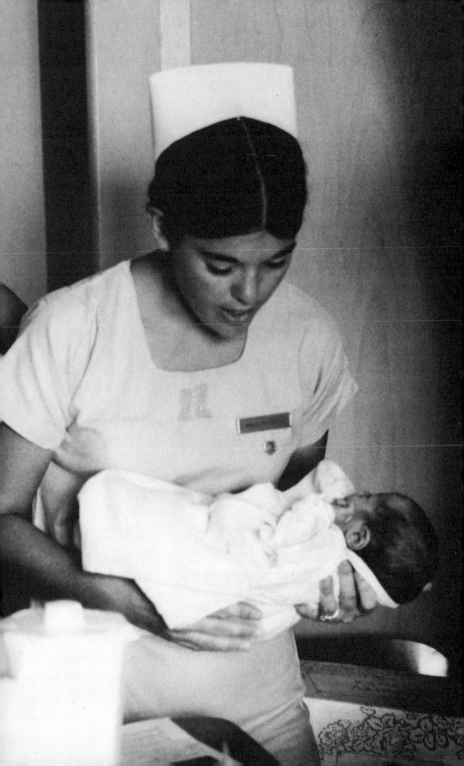

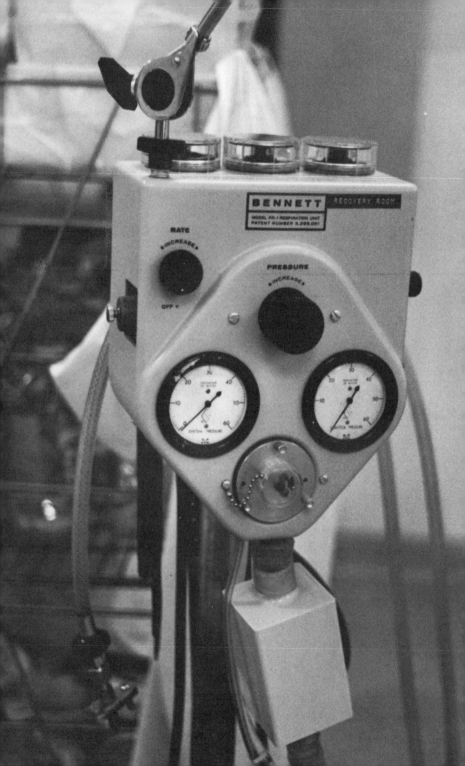

These "post-op" cases,
Lord,
remind me of puppets
attached to so many strings;
lifelines
to the I.V., the oxygen,
the catheters, the suction.

We seldom think about
our health
until it's gone or impaired;
we hold fast to our strings;
we're frightened and scared.

How many lifelines
are you holding on to,
Lord,
for each one, every day?
Hold our strings
around your finger.

"Give us this day
our daily bread."

Jesus,
I'm very human.

I want someone to notice me;
I want approval, Lord.

I don't want to work overtime
if nobody knows;
to warm an ice-cold bedpan
when he's too ill to complain,
to force fluids by the hour
through lips too weak to sip,
do passive exercises
on degenerative hips.

I'm trying to be a good nurse,
Lord,
but I want to be noticed.

I want my Father
"who sees in secret
to reward me"!

What a potpourri
of your peoples, Lord!

Negro, White, Filipinos,
every nationality. . .
strange,
seems here we feel
a unity.

Why can't we carry
this oneness
to the outside?
Why does it take pain
and suffering
to break the barriers
to unity?

. . . through suffering
our brotherhood
was purchased.

Help us, Jesus,
to love
our brothers.

As a child, I remember
it was a game
to close our eyes
and pretend
that we were blind;

and walk a few steps
and even run
in tall grass
where we knew we were safe,
and even then
we'd steal a glance
to be sure.

As I guide my patient
these few steps,
is he too remembering
how it was
to walk unafraid
and even run? . . .

His blindness is no game;
he has no chance
to steal a glance.

Lord,
grant him that "light
that shines
in the darkness."

Christ,
teach me
to be true to myself,

to know my goals
and limitations,
not to strive
to fulfill
false expectations.

Teach me
the value of loving
the sick,
the poor,
the bothersome,
the bore.

Teach me
that all men are equal;
teach me
to fulfill
your will.

A patient said to me
one day,
"You have a beautiful smile
Mrs. Gray."
My smile?! . . .
and then I realized,
her face
was paralyzed.

Another
said to me one day,
"Your voice is kindly
Mrs. Gray."
He sought a voice
that sounded kind,
for he
was blind.

Another patient
wrote me notes,
"What time of day is it
Mrs. Gray?"
That little note pad
was all she had;
she neither spoke nor heard
a word.

Sometimes
the smallest little thing
is everything!

Thank God
for the rumble
of meal carts.

The hustle back and forth
of brightly colored trays,
hot plates and salad plates;
at least three times a day
the call bells
get a rest!
Nearly everyone is happy

with the cuisine;
the monotony is broken
in the patient's routine.

I wish that once in a while
the diet staff could see
the smiles,
because they're genuine
and they'll be there again
with the next rumble!

Lord,
sometimes I think
you cater to nurses—
handing your gospel
on a silver platter!

We feed the hungry,
give drink to the thirsty,
comfort the afflicted
and tend Christ
depicted in pain;
but
what does this matter
if
feelings of grandeur
place humility
out of reach?
if
we mistake our pebbles
for the beach!

Remind us, Lord,
"that he who exalts himself
shall be humbled."

The "graveyard shift"
they call it;
it's supposed to be quiet!
We haven't stopped
since midnight!

Three emergencies—
why do they pick the nights
for their accidents and fights?
Oh Lord,
why am I complaining?
Did you check the time
before you healed?

Forgive my selfishness.
Help me to love,
for "we know not
the hour."

Lord,
OBS is a happy floor,
a smile in every room.

Mothers
still in their teens,
others,
the second time around.
The lady with twins
after ten years
of hoping and praying!

It's so pleasant,
Lord,
to work up here.

Thanks for the break;
thanks for birth and babies;
thanks for love and life.

For "Love" and "Life"!

Twelve hours in labor!
Christ,
that's a long time.

"The woman
when she has been in labor,
forgets the pain
for the joy
that her child is born."
Help her, Lord,
to remember your promise!

Right now
she is wondering
why she ever decided
to have a child!

Lord,
deliver her.

Row upon row
of tiny bassinets;
pink and blue
bundles of joy!
They sure have healthy lungs!

It feels almost mysterious,
Lord,
to hold them in my arms . . .
so helpless and dependent,
so frail and fragile;
yet
ultimate perfection
in six little pounds!

Can't help but wonder
what the future holds
for each one. . . .

Yet even more I ponder,
that each one
holds our future!

Fifteen young years, a mother;
just a child
giving birth to a child. . . .

Like a flower
tossed in the wind
brings forth a new bud;
not understanding
the beauty of life.

Somewhere waiting,
a loving heart,
an empty womb,
the vase
to receive her bouquet.

In this way
"He makes her who was barren
a joyful mother
of children."

The unfinished symphony,
the sculpture
knocked from the pedestal
just before
the final touch. . . .

though never come to birth,
never living,
never dies
but continues its creation
in the heart
of its creator.

And so the symphony,
the masterpiece,
the stillborn child! . . .
lives eternally
in a mother's loving heart;

in the heart
of its Creator.

"I have not lost
any which you gave me."

Not the abortion case!
What about my convictions?
I wasn't going to nurse
"these" patients!

But she's here, Lord,
and she's ill. . .
maybe ill in body
and even worse
in soul.
Maybe she's sorry;
maybe she wishes it were
only a dream. . .
but it's too late!

"Lord,
be merciful;
we know not what we do!"

When does "life" begin?

One claims
at the moment of conception;
another,
the last trimester
of gestation;
another,
at birth. . . .

Theologians tread lightly,
Scientists search endlessly;
Society demands decisions.

If
we have no answer
to
"when does life begin?"
dare we think
we have the answer
to
"when life should end"?

"Render to God
the things
that are God's."

Why did she have to die?
Those three young children
motherless,
and her husband. . . .

Oh Lord,
help him through this misery;
help him to accept;
he is so alone;
let him feel your presence.

Ease these first hours
as only you can;
give him strength
to give his children.

"In his weakness,
make him strong."

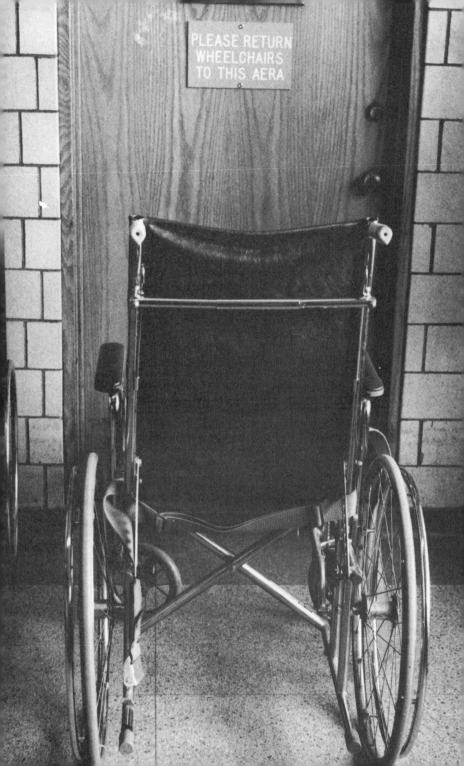

PLEASE RETURN
WHEELCHAIRS
TO THIS AERA

Are we "just"
when we decide
to hide the truth
from the terminally ill?

Perhaps
it is his right
to be allowed to speak
of his illness,
his fears,
his anxieties,
his family

or
perhaps he would speak
of his relief,
of his joy,
of his peace . . .

but we decide
he shall not speak
at all.

Are we just?

Disease,
you have no manners,
no respect
for your victim.

You move in
uninvited
to the wrong house
at the wrong time,
to destroy all his work,
to spend all his savings,
to dwell like a lord
and to conquer
by the maliciousness
of death.

But what defeat
your victory
to the man who knows that
Christ
"is the Resurrection
and the Life"?

If we know,
if we truly believe
that life
is a gift
to be recalled—
to be replaced
by the everlasting gift
of eternal love,
why do we cling
to a loved one . . .
surround him in tears
and intrude
on his final moments,
those precious moments
that he lives only once?

Should we not
look on
in silent awe

as he lives
the most vivid reality
of life?
death!

I

His doctor
broke the news today;
just two more months
to live!

"It can't be so!
Why me!
Why me?
I have so much yet
to give.

"This must be wrong!
I can't have only
that long! . . . .
It can't be true.

"I hate you,
God!
I hate,
I hate,
I hate!"

II

Then,
restless days
of endless quests. . . .

"Hey, God!
I need some time;
I want some time;
I want to finish living.

"I'll do something great
if it's not too late!

"Do you hear?
If you're there?!. . ."

III

The days pass on,
the sleepless nights;
he's only aware
of darkness. . . .

His wife stays near,
He feels her tender, loving care
but cannot share;
his mind
an endless turmoil. . . .

"What can I do?
I must resign;
I must resign . . .
tomorrow!"

IV

"Okay, God
you win;
you win!

"It would be all right
to die tonight.
Just look after my family.
Help them to see
this is best for me.
It's harder for them
than for me!

"Stay close to me, my God;
stay close!
I have no fear
when you're near . . ."

I'm just about
to begin my day;
thought I'd better
stop first
and pray.

Wonder what
the wards will bring.
New post-ops
among other things. . . .

Is Mrs. Brown
still around?
It's a crime how
she holds that bed;
all her pains
are in her head!

Sorry, Lord,
to think that way.
You'd better put love
in my heart
today.

Your chapel's so peaceful
it tempts me to stay,
but the floor's extra busy
today.

I just have a minute
on the way to the lab;
have to take
what I can grab.

You understand.

Can you give me a hand,
or take mine? . . .

Thanks
for a few minutes
in the middle
of the day.
I'm really grateful
for a moment
to pray.

I know you accept
my work
as my prayer;
but I need
to spend some time
with you, here. . . .

Just ducked in
on the way to lunch.
Sorry
I'm always
in such a rush!

Come down with me
to the cafeteria;
shop-talk
borders on hysteria
but
join us anyway.

Some of us
pray that way,
okay?

It's me;
I have to cry
for a minute!
Her suffering and pain
pushed my strength
to the limit.

I've got to go back
to hold her hand;
Will you give me
the courage
to stand?

Thanks, Jesus!

Another shift over;
I nursed quite a few
and listening took time.
It cost me
some criticism
but I didn't mind.

I thought
I would serve you
better
that way;
I trust
I did your will
today. . . .

The tears of gratitude
when a loved one recovers,
the tears of loneliness,
the tears of sorrow,
the tears of relief
when one discovers
his illness is curable.

The tears of frustration
to the new paralytic,
the tears of suffering and pain,
the tears of happiness,
the tears of helplessness,
to be listed as critical;
the tears of joy
when a mother learns
her little boy
will walk again . . .

are the tears
that flow into
the sea
of life.

NEEDED:
Nurses

QUALIFICATIONS:
Willingness
to love,
to understand,
to be compassionate
kind and gentle.

To be ready to work overtime,
to listen,
to comfort,
to smile and to support.

To suffer
and to cry (in private),
to serve the Lord your God
with all your heart,
with all your soul,
with all your mind,
with all your will.

SALARY:
"a hundredfold."